MW01462996

Today's Life

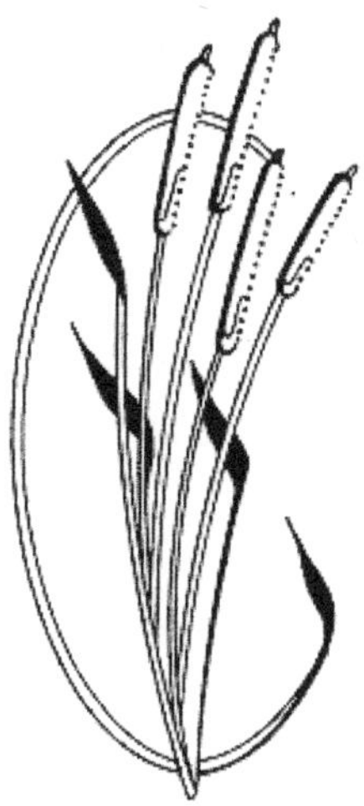

Today's Life

by

Ann

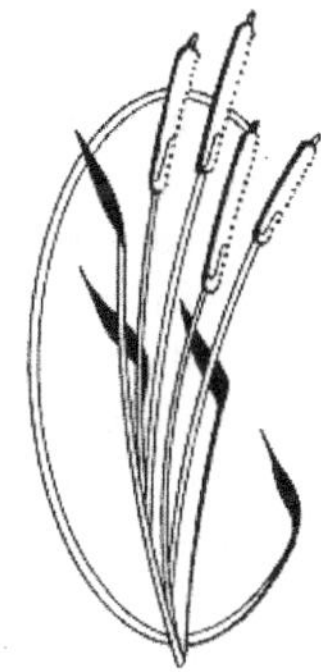

Senior Publisher

Steven Lawrence Hill Sr.

Awarded Publishing House

ASA Publishing Company

Established Since 2005

ASA Publishing Company
An Accredited Business with the Better Business Bureau
105 E. Front St., Suite 101 , Monroe, Michigan 48161
United States of America
www.asapublishingcompany.com

Book: Today's Life
Date Published: 08.22.2012
Edition: 1 *Trade Paperback*
Book ID: ASAPCID2380610
ISBN: 978-1-886528-85-7
Library of Congress Cataloging-in-Publication Data

This book was published in the United States of America.
State of Michigan

A Publisher Trademark Title page

Table of Contents

Poetry

Acknowledgements

Thank you, Steven Hill,
For being here for me and the girls.
For the help, for being my friend,
For getting my book out there for me.

My Mom, Dad, Don Kahler, Stepmom, and my Stepdad.

All the kids: Jackie Marie, Sylvia Anne, My Son who God took home with him. God needed him there, 22 years he has been there. Emily Rose, Tammy Jean and the sons we help take care of, Tony and Royce .

To all my family that has passed on:

.My son,
.Uncle Buddy,
.Uncle Speedy Futrel,
.My Grandpa, My Grandma
.My Aunt Sally,
.Uncle Earl Fairbairn,
.Razora Dusseau
.Jonna Dusseau,
.Uncle Michael Dusseau
.Gregory Alan Hopkins

To all my friends that has passed on in misfortunate causes:
Steven's mother who had a misfortunate stroke,
and his father because of a health situation.
Sue, from school together, passed on in her sleep (unexplained).
Mary, who left us from Aids,
Carrie, by a misfortunate suicide,
Tony, by another misfortunate suicide,
and John from today's addictions of drugs.
Pat from depression,

and Don in a vehicle accident.
My best friend for 14 years, Barb who went home to be with **God** in 2014; it was health issues.

My sister, Tammy Marie, who is still missing.
To my home church
First United Methodist Church of Monroe, Michigan for all the prayers and help. For caring about me and what happens to me. Thank you and I love you all.

To all of my family
That has been there for me, for loving me for the way I am.

To all my AA family
That has been here for me,
Helped me stay clean, loved me for just being me.

To Sandy and Kathy
For taking me in and helping me get on the right way of life,
I will always pray for you and family.
You two have really blessed my life.

To all my friends
That have been here for me; old and new.

To all the people that believe learning is hard, do not give up. It might be hard but you can do it, just do it your way and you will do it.

Today's Life

by

Ann

Love

Is something that is hard to understand,
But we all want it in life.
Why do we, or why do we think we need it, or can have it.
We want love because we want someone to say that they care about you.
And to know that someone is on your side.
And always be here for you.

Why?

Why is the sky on top?
Why do we do the things that we do as people, good or bad?
Why do we go through tests in life?
Why are we in today's world and not the past?
Why is there good and bad days?
Why do we get things and then lose them?
Why do we get people in our life and then lose them.
Why? Because everything has a time and place and we just got to do it,
Right the first time.

Hope

Hope, why do we?
Hope, why we ask for nice things.
Hope, why do we dream for good times in life?
Hope is something that we as people just do.
Hope for a good job.
Hope for children.
Hope for the best in life.
Hope that all dreams can come true in life.

The Gift of Love

The gift of **love.**
The gift of **life.**
The gift of **joy.**
The gift of **hope.**
The gift of **happiness**.
The gift of **children.**
The gift of a **mate.**

If you have all this you are **blessed?**
ALWAYS

Do not forget that.
Do not over**look the little things** because that is where your blessing is.

A Lady

Sitting at a bus stop.
Do we look or just keep going with today life?
Do you know if she needs help, or do you know if she eats today,
Or you know if she had a bath today and or place so she can sleep.
Or is it just because we do not have time or care
we got our life?

So what does that make **us?**

Today's World

If today's world would be better, If **people would care.**
If today's world would be better, If we took **care of things** so it stayed pretty, but we don't.
Today's world would be better, If we **grew nice things**, but we try down and just don't care.
If today's world would be better, If we **love and care for the animal**.
But a lot of people **just kill them.**
If today's world would be better, If people would **help people** but they try to bring them down and keep them there and have no **bad feelings** about it when they do it.

People that could be an Angel

People that come **out of nowhere**.
People that just want to **help with nothing back**.
People that will just walk up and **give you a coat.**
People that will just walk up and **feed you** or give you money to **get something** to **eat.**
People that will just stop and **help someone that is hurt.**
People that will just take **time to say hello.**
People that will just take care of someone and they do not need to be **blood family** to help.
People that will **help you get up** when you fall.
People that take time to **help older people**.
People that will care if you are **okay or not,** If you having a **good day** or **bad day.**

Children that live in Today

The children in today.
They can trust **NO ONE**.
They cannot have things because someone will try to **kill them over it**.
They cannot love because they think **they will get hurt**.
They cannot play like in the past because most people will go off and say it is **something else.**
They just want to be **kids and cannot.**
They cannot help people because it will look bad **they will still be picked on.**
Why can't we just be children and **have fun like the past,**
Like making things and **having fun doing it.**

God Sees

God sees if we are **good.**
God sees if we are **bad.**
God sees if we **care.**
God sees if we do **not care**.
God sees if we **help someone**.
God sees if we do **not help someone**.
God sees if we are **for Him**.
God sees if we are **for our self.**
God sees if we are **good to our family**.
God sees if we are **not good to our family**.
God sees if we **live right.**
God sees if we do **not live right.**
So how do you want **God to see you?**

The Best Things in Life

The best things in life are free, or are they?
The best things in life, is your time.
The best things in life, is helping someone.
The best things in life, is helping someone that is hurt.
The best things in life, is having a family.
The best things in life, is having the right to say yes or no.
The best things in life, is having the right to have the best.
The best things in life, is having the right to have your side said.
The best things in life, is having the right to take time to see all the flowers and be happy.

A Mate

A mate is someone that **spends time** with you . . .
A mate is someone that is always there for you.
A mate is someone that is there in the **good times.**
A mate is someone that is there in the **bad times**.
A mate is someone that loves you, not what you can **do** or **give** them, that they **just love you.**
A mate is someone that is here to spend the time with you and helps your **dreams** come true.
A mate does understand you and helps when you need it.
A mate is someone that helps you with the **children.**
A mate is someone that cares about how you feel and your **likes** and **dislikes.**
A mate is the one you want to **spend the rest of your life** with and you do not **see anyone but your mate.**

Our Children

Our children are the **light of my life.**
Our children are seeing **me when I was little.**
Our children are watching them in **their new things.**
Our children are like seeing a child **eat candy for the first time**.
Our children are like watching them **ride a bike for the first time.**
Our children are always like seeing them sleep, you look so **peaceful and happy.**

This poem is for all of you.
Thank you for letting me be your mother,
Jackie, Sylvia, Tammy and Emily

A Pup

A pup named **Lady,**
A pup that took **my heart the first time** I seen her.
A pup that is **happy** and **playful.**
A pup that is letting you know that **she loves you.**
A pup that gives you kisses and will **watch you when you work.**

Thank you, Lady
I love you – Your mom

P.S. You keep me going.
Keep up the good work.

A Father

A father, I do not know what it is like.
A father I wish I did know.
A father I wish that got to spend time with me.
A father that left when I was little.
A father that did not see me grow up and be a lady.
A father that I pray every night for.
A father that someday I hope to see.
A father that someday will get to know me.
A father that someday I want to meet my husband too, he is a good man.
A father that someday will meet his grandkids and spend time with them.

I do love you, you are my father.

To my father,
Don Kahler

A Mother

A mother is someone that **cares for you**.
A mother is someone that is there for **you when you fall.**
A mother is someone that **teaches you about new things.**
A mother is someone that **helps you** understands you **when you do not.**
A mother is someone that cares about how you or **what you need.**
A mother is someone that makes things with you and **wants to spend time with you.**
A mother is someone that watches you and **hopes the best for you always**.
A mother is someone that **will always be there for you**.
A mother is someone that **helps you with homework**.

This poem is to Jackie, Sylvia, Tammy and Emily

This poem is for you only mother,

My mother, things are not what they seem. I wish it all was this way but it is not. We do not talk or spend time together, I have not seen her in over 8 years, sometimes there is bad blood in ways and things we all do. I have nothing to say about my mother but I do forgive her and still love her. She will always be my mother.

My Mother

My mother is one that cares.
My mother is one that teaches you things.
My mother is one that will care but has a hard time showing it.
My mother is one that will be a friend if you let her.
My mother is one that likes making a cake and getting to eat it too.

My mother just needs to be loved.
My mother, I just wanted to talk to her but it was hard for me.
My mother, when you do not feel good and will give you a hug and a cup of soup at the same time.
My mother, thank you for being my mother.

Love your child,
Ann

This poem is for my big sister,
Tammy Kahler

My Big Sister

My big sister is one to look up to.
My big sister is one that will help me.
My big sister is one that will help me lean.
My big sister is one that will play a game with me.
My big sister is one that will play with me first.
My big sister is one that cares and will keep me out of trouble.

My big sister is one that will cut your hair for you.
My big sister would help me with my homework and make sure you get it right.
My big sister will try things first so if she gets in trouble you know not to do it too.
My big sister will let you know how to act the right way or you will pay for it in the long end.

I do love you, and thank you big sis.
Love, Ann

A Dark Side of The Family

A dark side is that which is not always as it seems.
A dark side is that which is nice on the outside but in the inside something else.
A dark side is yelling.
A dark side is being hit.
A dark side is kids being left by themselves while Mom or Dad is getting high.
A dark side is that the kids do not eat tonight so you can get high.
A dark side is kids playing outside at 2:00am so you do it in the house while they are outside by their self.
A dark side is that you die because of getting high so what happens to the kids?
A dark side is rape in the family.
A dark side is that there is killing in the family.
A dark side is that the kids got your stuff and tried it and die because of it.
A dark side is that people are for them so what about the little ones? All they did was be born.
So you are not just hurting yourself, you are hurting the kids from growing up the right way.
If they grow up at all.

This is for all the lost kids out there.
God watch over and bless you.
You are not by yourself!

My Grandpa

My grandpa was my dad to me.
My grandpa did love me and care.
My grandpa did teach me things.
My grandpa was there for me if I needed him.
My grandpa showed me how to fish and clean it.
My grandpa he had time to show me things.
My grandpa always spent time with me.
My grandpa would always have time to talk to me.
My grandpa was there in good times.
My grandpa was there in bad times.
My grandpa that I do love and miss so much.
My grandpa the thing I miss the most is me getting to talk to him and us going for walks together, I love you Grandpa!

I miss you!

Love your grandchild,
Ann

My Grandma

My grandma was nice to me.
My grandma did care about me.
My grandma would play games with me.
My grandma showed me things with cooking.
My grandma liked making things and I did learn that from her.
My grandma liked nice things so I would make things for her on all the holidays.
My grandma liked flowers.
My grandma and I did spend time together.
But when I got older I did not see her that much.

But I do still love her she will always be my grandma!

Love your grandchild,
Ann

The Chair

One day some people noticed a chair that was thrown in the dumpster 4 times by the owner. The owner mumbled, 'Why don't this chair just stay in the dumpster! I know what, I'll break it, and then maybe, just maybe, no-one will want it until the trash truck comes and take it away with all the other garbage. When the owner left, the people watching started taking turns examining the chair.

One said: This is a nice chair, but I do have any use for it right now.
Another said: This is a solid chair, must have took a lot to try to break it! It's a shame it's the wrong color.
The 3rd person was with child: And the child said, 'Mommy look at that chair, aren't you going to go get it?!"

So the third person looked at it, examined it, studied it, and said: "This is a beautiful chair, although it looks like it was used as someone's footstool. But I believe it has more potential in it than it was used for. So the third person with child took it home and began to notice that this antique chair was valuable and precious because even with 3 legs left to stand, it refused to fall over, and that those legs were made of gold under all that scarred up wood.

Now when the owner heard that the chair was indeed more valuable than anything in the house, the owner becomes furious, and tried to take it back. Even tried to find a receipt for the chair, but the chair was first discovered at a yard sale, and we all know that yard sales don't carry receipts.

Goes to show you, that one man's trash, is another man's treasure. Even if it relates the chair in human form.

Steven Hill gave me this on 8/31/2001 August 31st, 2001 and we got married that same year. We were married for over 8 years. I thank him for loving me and caring for me and wanting to be a part of my life and the girl's lives, Tammy and Emily.

Love, Melissa Carte

P.S. Thank you for making my life happy and full.

With permission of Steven Lawrence Hill Sr.

Children

Why do we not see them smile?
Why do we not see them be happy?
Why do we not see them just be kids?
Why do we not see them just have fun?
Why do we not care or help the child no more?
Why do we not take time to be here for the child?
Why do we not take time to listen to the child?
Because we are more important than the child?

That is so sad . . .

My Stepdad

To my Stepdad that I really don't know.
To my Stepdad that I would like to know.
To my Stepdad, that I hope the past stays in the past.
To my Stepdad, that I tried to be a friend but it did not work.
To my Stepdad that I wanted to talk to and spend time with but it did not work.
To my Stepdad that I did try to be a friend to you, I did try, but it did not work . . .

So I did try in this, so God bless you and that your life is happy and good!

Love your stepchild,
Ann

Our Mail Lady

Our mail lady is always being nice.
Our mail lady always has something nice to say.
Our mail lady has time to make you feel good if you had a bad day.
Our mail lady has time to **see** Lady and say hi and give a goody; she looks forward to seeing you.
Our mail lady has time to care for someone with a good heart.
Our mail lady, I wanted to tell you, thank you for caring, for being here and having a good heart.
Our mail lady: **God bless you and God does love YOU.**

From our family, The Hill's
To you, Our Westland Mail Lady!

Have a blessed day.

Just Because

Just because I did it.
Just because I want to.
Just because I feel like it.
Just because I have that right to.
Just because I said so.
Just because I want it done.

This is for the ones, just do it to be nice . . .

A Pest

Is someone or something
That is here when you do not want them there.
That is there and will not leave.
That is always in the way. Why?
That is the same one that will help too.
That is why it is hard to get rid of them.
That is the way that it is, just don't know why.
That is today's thing.

A Melissa Saying

What are we here for, why?
Or is it a dream and we just cannot get up...
Then on some days it seems like we are not there...
Then days we are here and cannot move at all...

—Sister Melissa

Childhood

Childhood, everything is new.
Childhood, everything is cool.
Childhood, everything is doing things with your friends.
Childhood, everything is done for the first time.
Childhood is everything like making friends.
Childhood is like having a birthday party.
Childhood is like thinking we are all that.

Then we grow up.

Cindypoo

Cindypoo was my best friend.
Cindypoo was here for me all the time.
Cindypoo was the one that played with me.
Cindypoo was the one that would give me kisses to make me feel better.
Cindypoo was the one that would watch TV with me.
Cindypoo was the one that would look at me with sad eyes.
Cindypoo was my first dog.
Cindypoo was a good dog.
Cindypoo was my friend.
Cindypoo! I miss you and I do love you! Sleep well my friend!

To Old Friends

Old friends, we had fun.
Old friends, we had to try anything one time.
Old friends, we said and acted like we was cool.
Old friends, you could not tell us nothing, we know it all.
Old friends, we said we would not grow up.
Old friends, we said that everything would be the same and not change. **Yea, right.**
Old friends, we said we would not get old. **Yea, right.**
Old friends, we said that we had and know all.
Old friends, but we did not know it all.
Old friends, we were just learning.
Old friends, so we are old now.
Old friends, so we had kids.

Pay Day

Pay day got paid.
Pay day, paid the rent.
Pay day on the bills.
Pay day on storage.
Pay day, need food.
Pay day, need coat for the kids.
Need blood? No money left.
But God always takes care of us.
We always make it.
And He sees all our needs are met!

Always,... Thank You, Lord.

The Little People in Today

Little people in today; we want good jobs
Little people in today; us want-to-want nice things
Little people in today; we want to go to new places
Little people in today; we want to go on outing
Little people in today; we have hopes and dreams too
Little people in today; we want the best for our family's too
Little people in today; we want people to talk to us and be nice too
Little people in today; we want the right to be happy
Little people in today; we want the right to have our peace and say too and heard
Little people in today; we want the big people to know we are out here
Little people in today; we want the world to know just because we are little people we have a heart too
Little people in today; we do have rights too
Little people in today; we want to be trusted right not miss used
Little people in today; we just want to live and be happy too
Little people in today; and not be judged for it
Little people in today; because we are the little people

God's Gift

God's gift is love.
God's gift is family.
God's gift is children.
God's gift is hope.
God's gift is understanding.
God's gift is faith.
God's gift is blessings.

God's gift is a new day.
God's gift is to forgive everyone.
God's gift is everyone to care for the ones in need.
God's gift is to help the hurting and care for them.

Test of Life

Are we **here** or not?
We got **high** and made it out alive.
We got **sick** and made it out alive.
We got **hurt** and made it out alive.
We got **shot** and made it out alive
We got left for **dead** and made it out alive.
We said no **one cared** but we made it out alive.
We said that test of life would **kill us.**
We did not think we would make it **out at all** but we did.

The Family House

The family house had happy times.
The family house had children playing all the time.
The family house had good holidays.
The family house had new babies all the time.
The family house had good homemade food to eat and new recipes to try.
The family house had more inside than just walls and doors.
The family house had people that care and family that had love.
So why did they tear it down when I was 10 years old? It was a good house.
I miss the family house.

The *Here* and *Now* Children

The here and now children,
Have single parents.
The here and now children,
Have to live with grandparents.
The here and now children,
Have no one to care for them, no parents at all.
The here and now children,
Have no one to love them.
The here and now children,
Just don't care.
The here and now children,
Just don't have time.
The here and now children,
Just do not want them, but have them.
The here and now children,
So this makes the children.
The here and now children,
That hurts.
The here and now children,
Be mean.
The here and now children,
Not care.
The here and now children,
See nothing for them.
The here and now children,
See no hope for them.
The here and now children,

So they do bad too.
The here and now children,
So they have anger.
The here and now children,
Such bad attitudes.
The here and now children,
So some will cause death to some.
The here and now children,
So some are out of control.
The here and now children,
So some have no guidance.
The here and now children,
So some have power.
The here and now children,
So some have no power.
The here and now children,
So some have will to go on.
The here and now children,
So some have no will left.
The here and now children,
So some live with guilt for being born.
The here and now children,
So some have no leadership.
The here and now children,
So some have no mentors.
The here and now children,
So some have no respect.
The here and now children,
So some are just suffering.
The here and now children,
So some have no values.
The here and now children,
So it makes it hard for today's kids.
The here and now children,
So who helps them?

The here and now children,
I feel so bad for all of them.

May **God** keep his hand on all of them?
May **God** bless them and give them a good life.
May **God** show them the good side of life.

Take Time

Take Time to care.
Take Time to love your mate.
Take Time to have fun.
Take Time to see new things.
Take Time to learn new things.
Take Time to eat new things.
Take Time to spend time with your kids.
Take Time to spend time with your grandkids.
Take Time to make new things.
Take Time to read a good book.
Take Time to watch a good movie.
Take Time to see an old friend.
Take Time to sit at a park and see and watch the birds and the squirrels.
Take Time just to rest.
Take Time to go to a new place.
Take Time to do things, to care and do something for yourself.

Family Test

Have a day, all you want to do is see a good movie,
And can't see it.
Every 5 minutes it is something else.
Why is that? When do we just do something for us?
Yea right.
Or does it seem like everything you do goes the other way,
But the way you wanted.

Little Children

Little Children,
Are so cute.
Little Children,
Are so funny.
Little Children,
Are so happy.
Little Children,
Are so much fun.
Little Children,
Are so into new things.
Little Children,
Are so into seeing new things.
Little Children,
Are into trying new things.
Little Children,
If only we stayed Little.
Little Children,

But we all grow up.
Little Children,
But we all have dreams, so make them come true.
Little Children,
But we always do not see, and do what our dreams are.

People Think They Know You

People think they know you,
But they do not.
People think they know you,
But they think they do.
People think they know you,
Why do they say or do that?
People think they know you,
But today they think and say a lot.
People think they know you but it is not true.
People think they know you, so why do people try to stop you?

Not me, I keep going.

The Walk Author

The walk, was a 5 minute walk.
The walk, but I got lost and it was a long walk.
The walk, I find the place that I was going to.
The walk, it was a 20 minute walk.
The walk, but I thank **God** that I made it here.
The walk, and I thank **God** I do not have to walk home.
The walk, thank you for your blessing.

The Rose

The rose that was a bud.
The rose that is growing.
The rose that made it through the cold.
The rose that makes it through the freeze.
The rose that stays alive.
The rose, but then I pick it.
The rose and then it started to die.
The rose and then it did dry out.
The rose the way things grow.
The rose, **red** and pretty.

The Work Day

The work day, it did not seem like I would get to work.
The work day, I was ready to go, but one thing, other things, then something else.
The work day, it was a long day. But I did make it to work.
The work day, and I did make it home.
The work day, I did have to see where they are going.
The work day, and the day is ending.
The work day, it turns out to be an okay day, still here, still alive.

Thank you, Lord

Some People

Some people; act like they are all that like they are better than us
Some people; they act like they run the world
Some people; they act like if you do not do what they say, you get hit or killed
Some people; they are the boss of the world
Some people; they are the boss of you
Some people; they act like we are noting, but to be hit and used
Some people; this is to the ones that get hit or used
Some people; you have rights to, to be happy, loved, cared about, not hit, to look nice, to have nice things
Some people; to some people that will take care of your rights, the way GOD wants you to be cared for

A Pot of Soup Family

1 cup of love.
1 cup of hope.
1 cup of understanding.
1 cup of caring.
1 cup of time.
4 cups of **God**.
1 cup of Dad.
1 cup of kids.
1 cup of Lady, the family pup.
1 cup of hugs and kisses.
1 cup of prayers.
1 cup of spending time as a family.

This makes a good pot of soup.
And it keeps you going.
And makes a blessed family.

A Cherokee Indian Woman

A Cherokee Indian woman, she had a good marriage.
A Cherokee Indian woman, she had good kids.
A Cherokee Indian woman, she had a good place to live.
A Cherokee Indian woman, she had good food to eat.
A Cherokee Indian woman, she had good ideals in life that worked.
A Cherokee Indian woman, she had a green hand when it came to plants, they would grow and be pretty.
A Cherokee Indian woman, she had dreams and they come true.
A Cherokee Indian woman, she had a gift in prayer, she would pray and it would come to pass.

The Cold Day

The Cold Day, it's a day for hot soup.
The Cold Day, it's for a good movie.
The Cold Day, it's for a good book to read.
The Cold Day, it's for a game to play.
The Cold Day, it's good for a hot cup of tea.
The Cold Day, it's for a good nap.
The Cold Day, it's good cleaning too or cleaning the house.

Kids Play

Kids Play, in the pool in the summer.
Kids Play, in the sandbox in the summer.
Kids Play, in the backyard and see and do new things.
Kids Play, in a cold day.
Kids Play, in the bugs.
Kids Play, in the plants.
Kids Play, in the snow.
Kids Play, and having fun.
Kids Play, in making new things.

The 911 Poem

The people in 911.
The children in 911.
The family pets in 911.
To the people that are still alive.
To the people that die.
To the ones that lost loved ones.
To the ones that do miss them.
To the ones that had dreams that did not come true.

You are not forgotten

The Parents

The Parents, we try to care for them.
The Parents, we try to love them.
The Parents, we try to show them we can help.
The Parents, we are always there for them.
The Parents, we do not want to see them get old.
The Parents, we do not want to see them sick.
The Parents, we do not want to see them die.

The In-Laws

The In-Laws, we want to get to know them.
The In-Laws, we want to spend time with them.
The In-Laws, we want to make them a part of the family.
The In-Laws, do we really get to know them?
The In-Laws, did we still try to make a part of the family.

The Guest

The Guest, we welcome them in.
The Guest, we will make a nice day for them.
The Guest, we hope they leave happy and say they had a nice day.
The Guest, we see them again but it is not the same.
The Guest, so did we change.
The Guest, so did they change.
The Guest, we do not want to say hi but we do to be nice and kind.
The Guest, but sometimes it does not work being nice and kind.

My Brother-In-Law

My Brother-In-law, I do not know you.
My Brother-In-law, I hope the best for you.
My Brother-In-law, I will and do pray for you.
My Brother-In-law, I did not meet you yet.
My Brother-In-law, I hope that you wake up.
My Brother-In-law, I hope you get off the streets.
My Brother-In-law, I hope you get yourself off of the bad things.
My Brother-In-law, I ask **God** to watch over you and take care of you.

The Happy Cooker

The Happy Cooker, we love to make new things.
The Happy Cooker, we love to eat what we cook.
The Happy Cooker, we love to let you eat with us.
The Happy Cooker, we try to make nice and good food.
The Happy Cooker, we make the food and want you coming back for more.
The Happy Cooker, if we mess up one, you will not know, we will dress it up.
The Happy Cooker, you will not find any leftovers with us.

The Family Meal

The Family Meal, it is the only time for some families to be together.
The Family Meal, it's time for a family talk.
The Family Meal, it is to see how your kids' day went.
The Family Meal, is when good things happened.
The Family Meal, it is time to say and do something new.
The Family Meal, to learn something new about each one.
The Family Meal, it's to eat good food and having good time doing it.

The Needy People Out Here

The Needy People Out Here, some have no hope.
The Needy People Out Here, some have no help.
The Needy People Out Here, some just stop caring.
The Needy People Out Here, some just have no will to live no more.
The Needy People Out Here, people don't have time.
The Needy People Out Here, people don't want to help.
The Needy People Out Here, people act like we are nothing to them.
The Needy People Out Here, and the people that can help will not help.

The Users Out Here

The Users Out Here, they take from the ones that need it.
The Users Out Here, they take all your will to go on.
The Users Out Here, they are kind and take everything at the same time.
The Users Out Here, they have money and use it for things that are not good.
The Users Out Here, they will talk to you and if you do not have what they want.
The User's Out Here, they will just kill you off, you are little or nothing to them.
The Users Out Here, they act like you are nothing to them at all.

A Family Pains In Life

A Family Pains In Life, we have good pains like having a baby.
A Family Pains In Life, we have good pains like falling off a bike when we are trying to ride it.
A Family Pains In Life, we have bad pains like family getting sick.
A Family Pains In Life, we have bad pains like family that gets killed.
A Family Pains In Life, we have bad pains like family that is ran over by a drunk driver.
A Family Pains In Life, we have good pains like seeing someone in the family get married.
A Family Pains In Life, we have good pains like seeing the world and get paid for doing it.

"Thanksgiving" What is it?

Thanksgiving, What Is It? It means all families together.
Thanksgiving, What Is It? It means we all eat good that day.
Thanksgiving, What Is It? It means we all play games together.
Thanksgiving, What Is It? It means we spent time with the new kids or new babies.
Thanksgiving, What Is It? It means we catch up on old times.
Thanksgiving, What Is It? It means we thank **God** for a new year!
Thanksgiving, What Is It? It means we see the old loves that die.
Thanksgiving, What Is It? It means we see old friends and see how they're doing.

"Thanksgiving" What does it mean to homeless?

Thanksgiving, What Does It Mean To Homeless? It means a day with no food.
Thanksgiving, What Does It Mean To Homeless? It means a day to be cold.
Thanksgiving, What Does It Mean To Homeless? It means a day with no place to stay because they are filled up.
Thanksgiving, What Does It Mean To Homeless? It means a day that you might die because of the cold or freeze.
Thanksgiving, What Does It Mean To Homeless? It means you have no family to be with.
Thanksgiving, What Does It Mean To Homeless? It means you have no one to have a good day with.
Thanksgiving, What Does It Mean To Homeless? It means you have no mate to be with.

May God bless you and give you a place to be, to eat, to have heat, to have someone to care about you and love you for you.

The Misfits

The Misfits, people that talk or look at someone like they're better than them.
The Misfits, people that act like they are better than them.
The Misfits, it is someone that gets a new dog or cat for Christmas and by the end of January they are trying to give it away. **They do not have time.**
The Misfits, people get new thing and have the same in old, they do not bless someone they throw it out.
The Misfits, there is a place for everyone and everything but no one takes time to find it.
The Misfits, in some ways we all are misfits and things until someone wants you or it.

Christmas

Christmas, it is a time for families to get together
Christmas, it is a time for families to do stuff together.
Christmas, it is a time for new things for you.
Christmas, it is a time to eat Grandma's goodies and your aunt's dry ham.
Christmas, it is a time to do things for someone.
Christmas, it is a time to try or do new things.
Christmas, it is a time to see old people in the family and spend time with new babies in the family.
Christmas, so you have a good Christmas and be nice to someone you don't know this year! **Be a blessing**

Christmas, what about the homeless people!?

Christmas, what about the homeless people? They are in the cold.
Christmas, what about the homeless people? They are in the rain.
Christmas, what about the homeless people? They are not eating today.
Christmas, what about the homeless people? They are by themselves.
Christmas, what about the homeless people? They are not getting a gift.
Christmas, what about the homeless people? They are not sleeping in a bed.
Christmas, what about the homeless people? They are not by the Christmas tree with family: reading and singing.
Christmas, what about the homeless people? They are not with old friends or family **most die** on the street as a **no name**.

So please take time to help someone on the street. **That** is **Christmas**.

Friends

Friends are there in the good times.
Friends are there in the bad times.
Friends are there when you are sick.
Friends are there to play card games with.
Friends have time for you.
Friends, when you just want to talk.
Friends make some of your happy times.
Friends help you make good food for family and friends for the good times.

The Big Cities

The Big Cities are so fast.
The Big Cities are not into caring.
The Big Cities just don't have time.
The Big Cities, where you get lost in the rat race all the time.
The Big Cities, where we are just a number, not a name.
The Big Cities, why are you? We do not have time or will not help you at all.

The Little Towns

The Little Towns, you have nice people that care.
The Little Towns, when family was family, **we took care of our family**.
The Little Towns, when you needed help we **all worked together to help!**
The Little Towns, where we know our friends were friends and are there for us.
The Little Towns, where the food was good food, not store bought.
The Little Towns, where a cook-out was a cook-out with good food, fun, games, and good times.
The Little Towns, when you got sick everyone helped take care of you.
The Little Towns, with the stores you want to go in and spend time and money.

The Little Towns, where kids can be kids and have fun doing it.
The Little Towns, where old family people were taken care of by family **not homes.**

The Holidays

The Holidays are fun and you get to eat a lot.
The Holidays, to see new and old family.
The Holidays, to spend time with all the family.
The Holidays, to play games with all the kids.
The Holidays, to sing songs to all and just be happy.
The Holidays, to read a good book or do family things you do every year.
The Holidays, take time to help or see someone you do not know and be kind.

A Little Bookstore

A Little Bookstore, it is cute.
A Little Bookstore, it has a lot of books.
A Little Bookstore, it has nice people.
A Little Bookstore, it has people that want to help.
A Little Bookstore, it has fun times.
A Little Bookstore, it has good, hot coffee.
A Little Bookstore, it has some old and new things in it.
A Little Bookstore, it has understanding and caring people that come and go.

The Goody Two-Shoe People

The Goody Two-Shoe People, they think because they have more money.
The Goody Two-Shoe People, they think because they have a nicer home.
The Goody Two-Shoe People, they think because they have a nicer car.
The Goody Two-Shoe People, they think because they have the best of everything.
The Goody Two-Shoe People, they think because they have kids.
The Goody Two-Shoe People, they think because they are all that.

But if you do not love and care for others you can lose it all.

Then what are you? The little people with egg on your face.

I hope it is not you, if it is what does that say about **you?**

Not me. I want people to say that she is **nice**, and **caring**.

Why People Act The Way They Do

Why People Act The Way They Do, because they do not care.
Why People Act The Way They Do, because they think they are better.
Why People Act The Way They Do, because they do what they want and do not care how it **hurts** because they're all that.
Why People Act The Way They Do, because they are out for themselves, that's all.
Why People Act The Way They Do, because they just do not have time.

"God" What He Means to Me?

"God" what He means to me, He saves me, I thank you God!
"God" what He means to me, He loves me, I thank you God!
"God" what He means to me, He cares about me, I thank you God!
"God" what He means to me, He takes care of my needs, I thank you God!
"God" what He means to me, He makes my things I *Pray* happen, I thank you God!
"God" what He means to me, He makes everything go the right way, I thank you **God**!

The Way I Want People to See Me

The way I want people to see me, take time to say hi.
The way I want people to see me, take time to help someone.
The way I want people to see me, take time to help the hurting.
The way I want people to see me, take time to give a meal.
The way I want people to see me, take time to hear what those have to say.
The way I want people to see me, take time to just care I do not need to know your name.
The way I want people to see me, take time to help the children.

Holidays, Why?

Holidays, Why do people feel so bad?
Holidays, Why do people try to kill themselves?
Holidays, Why do people act nice because they do not act that way all the time?
Holidays, Why do they think they are better than others?
Holidays, Why do they spend so much money that they do not have?

Good Days

Good Days, when everything goes right.
Good Days, when everything is happy.
Good Days, when everything is clean and neat.
Good Days, when everything is cooked for you and all got to do is eat.
Good Days, when all you got to do is read a good book or just sleep.

Bad Days

Bad Days, nothing goes right.
Bad Days, you cannot get it all done.
Bad Days, any and everything that could happen will.
Bad Days, everyone can and will be mean.
Bad Days, everyone can and will say mean things to you.

Stress, Why?

Stress, Why? It is a part of life.
Stress, Why? You cannot live without it.
Stress, Why? It is in every day when you get up.
Stress, Why? Because someone will give you it.
Stress, Why? Because someone always thinks they are better than you.
Stress, Why? Because someone says they do it better than you.

Depression

Depression makes you cry.
Depression makes you sleep all day.
Depression makes you not care at all.
Depression makes you not want to live no more.
Depression makes you act mean to people.
Depression makes you say mean things to people.

The Family Storm

The Family Storm is when something bad happens.
The Family Storm is when you cannot pay your bills.
The Family Storm is when nothing goes right at all.
The Family Storm is when everything is being taken from you.
The Family Storm is when you think there is no hope left.

Over 40

Over 40, your hair is grayer.
Over 40, your skin is so hard.
Over 40, your hair is falling out.
Over 40, your teeth are coming out.
Over 40, your friend is TV, newspaper.

Kid's Test

Kid's Test, not being in, the kids think they're cool.
Kid's Test, not having any friends at all.
Kid's Test, not fitting in anywhere.
Kid's Test, not making good grades.
Kid's Test is getting picked on and do nothing about it.

Teen's Test

Teen's Test, do they smoke?
Teen's Test, do they take pills?
Teen's Test, do they cut themselves?
Teen's Test, do they drink?
Teen's Test, do they go to that party?
Teen's Test, do they go with bad kids?
Teen's Test, do they go to that bar?
Teen's Test, do they have sex?

Sister Melissa's way is cool,

Stay clean, stay right, stay nice, and stay in school and finish.

People

People, why are some people nice?
People, why do some people just not care?
People, why do some people take time to care for you and help you?
People, why do some people help feed people?
People, why do some people not help feed people?

Test

Test, why do we get things just to lose it?
Test, why do we work so hard to lose it all?
Test, why do we get people in our life to lose them again?
Test, why does it feel like sometimes we are by our self?
Test, why does it feel like sometimes we are losing our mind?
Test, why do we work to make money just to lose it again?
Test, why do we wish for things and lose them or never get them?

† My Heavenly GOD †

My Heavenly **God**, does He love me?
My Heavenly **God**, does He take care of me?
My Heavenly **God**, does He want my hopes and dreams come true?
My Heavenly **God**, does He have and want the best for me?
My Heavenly **God**, does He make my prayers come to pass?
My Heavenly **God**, does He put families together?
My Heavenly **God**, does He bless families that do care and help others?

† Heavenly Life †

Heavenly Life, has dreams.
Heavenly Life, has good life.
Heavenly Life, has understanding.
Heavenly Life, hope for the good.
Heavenly Life, has good times, all the time.
Heavenly Life, has nice and good places.
Heavenly Life, has good and nice people in it.

Little People in Today

Little people in today, we want good jobs too.
Little people in today, we want to do nice things too.
Little people in today, we want to go to nice places and outings too.
Little people in today, we have hopes and dreams too.
Little people in today, we want the best for our families too.
Little people in today, we want people to talk to us right and be nice too.
Little people in today, we want the right to be happy too.
Little people in today, we want the right to have our peace said and heard too.
Little people in today, we want the big people to know we are out there.
Little people in today, we want the world to know just because we are little people, we do have rights too.
Little people in today, we want to be treated right and not be miss used!
Little people in today, we just want to live and be happy too, and not to be judged for it.
Little people in today, because we are the little people.

Some People

Some people act like they are all that like they are better than us.
Some people, they act like they run the world.
Some people, they act like if you do not do what they say, you get hit or killed.
Some people, they act like they are the boss of the world.
Some people, they act like they are the boss of you.
Some people, they act like we are nothing but to be hit and used.
Some people, they are the ones that shall get hit and used but they are the ones doing it, they think they are cool but it is not cool to hip.
Some people, you have **rights** too, to be happy, loved, cared about. Not hit, to look nice, to have nice things, to someone that will take care of you right, the way **God** wants you to be cared for.

WHAT Is Today About?

What is today about? Most people just do not care.
What is today about? Most people do not know how to care.
What is today about? Most people do not love people.
What is today about? Most people do not have time.
What is today about? Most people do not talk to people.
What is today about? Most people do not help people in need!
What is today about? Most people just do not take time to do nothing only if it is for that one only.
What is today about? Most people, the new thing is to care for

yourself right.
What is today about? Most people that just makes me feel so bad for todays' kids.

The Stepfamily

The Stepfamily, **God** gives us family and He added more.
The Stepfamily, we could be one way and they might be another.
The Stepfamily, but **God** does what He feels is right.
The Stepfamily, we will be one color and they might be another.
The Stepfamily, we do learn together.
The Stepfamily, we do make a family together.
The Stepfamily, we get blessed together too.
The Stepfamily, and **God** takes care of all of us and makes that we have, what we need.

Jungle of Footprints in the Snow

Jungle of Footprints, how many people before me?
Jungle of Footprints, how did the footprints start?
Jungle of Footprints, where did they come from?
Jungle of Footprints, how was the one that made the same footprints able to make them the same?
Jungle of Footprints, why does no one clean it so there is not a
Jungle of Footprints, why do people make footprints in the snow?
Jungle of Footprints, do you even think of the people that made the footprints about their life?
Jungle of Footprints, why did they walk in the same place as me and make footprints?

The Wedding Day

The Wedding day, it is the happy day.
The Wedding day, it is the longest day.
The Wedding day, it is the day family and friends are there to see you two.
The Wedding day, it is full of good times.
The Wedding day, it is that you know that you two are now one forever.
The Wedding day, it is that God made you a family now.
The Wedding day, it is this day that is the start of the rest of your life as one.

Marriage

Marriage is when two people, one man and one woman become as one forever.
Marriage is that they want to spend the rest of their life together.
Marriage is that they help each other in their life's dreams.
Marriage is that they have children together and take care of them.
Marriage is that they go places together.
Marriage is that they do things together like go on a date.
Marriage is that they get old together and watch and play with their grandchildren.

Daughters

Daughters are to be loved.
Daughters are for you to take care .
Daughters are for you to teach how to cook, new and old family recipes.
Daughters are for you to teach how to take care of the family when you get old.
Daughters are for you to teach God to so they can teach their children.
Daughters are for you to teach them to love themselves and care for themselves.
Daughters are children wanting to grow up like their mother.

Emily Rose and Tammy Jean

The Rain

The Rain is good when it comes.
The Rain, it makes the food grow.
The Rain, it makes the flowers grow.
The Rain, it makes the plants grow.
The Rain, it cleans up everything.
The Rain, It waters the big old trees.
The Rain, I love to just watch it rain.
The Rain cools everything down.
The Rain, I just love the smell of the rain.

The Ice

The Ice is cold.
The Ice is hard to walk on.
The Ice, is and can hurt you.
The Ice, is and can cut you.
The Ice, is and can make you break a bone.
The Ice, is and can make you get in it and you cannot get out.
The Ice, sometimes you cannot see it.

Black Ice

Black Ice can make you get hurt.
Black Ice is hard to see.
Black Ice can and will make cars chash.
Black Ice can and will make you fall because of it.
Black Ice can and will make you lose someone in your family because of it.

The Fall

The Fall, grow good food.
The Fall, good times.
The Fall, good for an outside lunch.
The Fall, good for spending time with family.
The Fall, good for have fun in the yard.
The Fall, good for cleaning the yard.
The Fall, good for putting summer out and getting other things out.

My Saying

Just take one day at a time,
And do your best for that day,
And try to help someone.
To show that they are cared about.
Do not let anyone tell you cannot do it.
Just do it in your time and way if they do say something tell them that **God** loves you,
And they will stop and let you be.
Just do your best you, do it your way.

The Dream

The Dream makes you stay up.
The Dream makes you see other life.
The Dream makes you see good things.
The Dream makes you see bad things.
The Dream makes you see things that could be.

Bipolar

To all the people that live with bipoler,
I know it is hard at times but you will get thru it.
If you try hard you can do what your dreams are.
You can make them come real.
Do not give up, keep going.
You have to want it.
You tell your doctor how you feel,
And where you are so they can help you,
The right way, It might take some time but do not give up.
And do take your meds and listen to your doctor,
And you will do it.

I am, and I thank **God** for that and the people he put there to help me.
I am living my life not letting life run me.
All we can do is try our best and go from there.

My Gift of Prayer

My Gift Of Prayer, have helped the people I pray for.
My Gift Of Prayer, **God** does help them.
My Gift Of Prayer, **God** does hear my prayers.
My Gift Of Prayer, **God** does take care of their needs.
My Gift Of Prayer, **God** is there but you have to be in the right mind and pray.
My Gift Of Prayer, **God** is love and he does hear if you are really trying
My Gift Of Prayer, all the people I did and have prayed for did come to pass.

My, Our Pathway

My, Our Pathway, in the way you live.
My, Our Pathway, in the way you see people.
My, Our Pathway, in the golds you have in life.
My, Our Pathway, in the way you and **God** talk.
My, Our Pathway, in the way you help and care.
My, Our Pathway, in the way you love and care for your family.
My, Our Pathway, in the way you have a relationship with your man.

Things

Things, people care about the things, but not the people.
Things, people care about how much money they have, not their family.
Things, people care about the house or helping someone. What about the homeless people?
Things, people the ones that need help and do not know how to ask for it.
Things, so **God** sends them to someone that will help them without asking for it.
Things, so what does that say about us?

The Wife

The Wife is the one that keeps the house warm and clean and full of good food.
The Wife is the one that takes care of all the children.
The Wife is the one that keeps the bedrooms fire broiling and hot all the time.
The Wife is the one that takes time to help others and get them what they need if they can.
The Wife is the one that makes sure everything is done.
The Wife is the one that prays for the family and tends to tell them good, not bad, the right thing to do.

The Bird, Heater

The Bird, Heater, we came home and
It was cold in the house.
The Bird, Heater, got in the heater,
We called the man and he said he would be out.
The Bird, Heater came out and he got the bird out,
It was still alive.
The Bird, Heater, and he put it in the street, the girls got a shoebox.
The Bird, Heater, then it flew in Mom and Dad's room,
Then in the bathroom.
The Bird, Heater, Dad took the bird to the door and the bird flew away.
The Bird, Heater, did not get cooked or die he or she is fine.

Moving

Moving, it is good.
Moving, it is learning more.
Moving, it is meeting new people.
Moving, it is going new places.
Moving, it is fun.
Moving, it is some work.
Moving, it is the time for new things.
Moving, it is for having good times.
Moving, it is for having fun doing it.

Joy Because

Joy because it is good.
Joy because it is fun.
Joy because it is cool.
Joy because it is wow.
Joy because the good part of life.
Joy because I want joy instead of sad things.
Joy because joy is hope for better things.

Crying

Crying, why we do not cry?
Crying, why only when someone dies?
Crying, why only when something bad happens?
Crying, why? Because we do not want people to say we do not
have a backbone, why? Yea right.
Crying, **God** give us tears for us in the
Happy times too.

Life

Life, why do we see like we're there?
Life, before, but we are going the way.
Life, but the same, always.
Life, cannot see life, too much going.
Life, on, no time, no fun, just trying.
Life, to make it, when does the fun come?

Be Happy

Be Happy because you are alive.
Be Happy because you have someone that cares.
Be Happy because you have a good outlook on life.
Be Happy because **God** gave you life and you should be happy because of that.
Be Happy because you have arms and legs.
Be Happy because you have a mind that works, some of us, our minds do not work good.
Be Happy because life is what you make of it.

Today's People

Today's people, some care and are there.
Today's people, some don't care and are out for themselves.
Today's people, some will help, and understand.
Today's people, some will do it for themselves and that is all.
Today's people, some people will see you need and help you.
Today's people, some people will see you need help and walk away, no time or they just do not care.
Today's people, so what happened to today's people?

Today Change to Live

Today change to live, the way we act.
Today change to live, the way we talk.
Today change to live, what we do in life.
Today change to live, what we wear.
Today change to live, how we wear it.
Today change to live, how we care for our body.
Today change to live, if we cut it up.
Today change to live, if we put holds in it.
Today change to live, if we mark it up.
Today change to live, if you care for yourself.
Today change to live, if you do not care for yourself.
Today change to live, so do you care for yourself?

Helping Hands

Helping Hands are there when you need them.
Helping Hands, Ex-hands always help when you need them.
Helping Hands, when you are working there are ones that help. **God** sends them to you.
Helping Hands, so **God** blessing you by sending them to you.
Helping Hands, so make time to thank **God** for all your blessing.
Helping Hands, so at the end of the day take time to see the work is done and your blessings.

Children Are Joy

Children Are Joy, children are happy.
Children Are Joy, children are carefree.
Children Are Joy, children know how to have fun.
Children Are Joy, children have a new look on life.
Children Are Joy, children have an open mind.
Children Are Joy, children are willing to learn new things.

The Girl

The Girl wants a good life.
The Girl wants a good family.
The Girl wants to do right things.
The Girl wants a nice place.
The Girl wants to have nice things.
The Girl wants to be cared for right.
The Girl wants **God** in her life,
And care's about **God**,
And is a good girl and has a good heart.
The Girl, I know that is trying her best to
Stay a good girl and stay alive.

A Little Bookstore

A little bookstore where you always feel welcome.
A little bookstore where someone is there to talk to.
A little bookstore where you can get a good book.
A little bookstore where someone will help you.
A little bookstore where someone will pray for you.
A little bookstore where there is always something going on.
A little bookstore, you feel bad,
You will feel better when you leave.
So the door is open and you are always welcome.

The Test of Time

The Test of Time, one day you get up and 20 years went by.
The Test of Time, one day you get up and you look old and have gray hair.
The Test of Time, one day you get up and see
Your kids have kids now.
The Test of Time, one day you get up and
You cannot do some things.
The Test of Time, one day you get up and half of your family went to **God**.
The Test of Time, one day you get up and
You cannot get around that much.
The Test of Time, one day you do not get up
You went to **God** too.
Do not waste the time you have left.

Receiving Your Gift

Receiving Your Gift, some will receive your gift by **God**.
Receiving Your Gift, some do not understand.
Receiving Your Gift, some will not take the gift.
Receiving Your Gift, some just did not believe.
Receiving Your Gift, some just did not care.
Receiving Your Gift, some did not have time.
Receiving Your Gift, some said that was funny.
Receiving Your Gift, but do you know the one that got the gift.
Receiving Your Gift, was the one that,
Was willing to take it and us the right way.

The Bird

The Bird, we came home from work.
The Bird, we seen it on the walkway.
The Bird, one of our girls, Tammy, picked her up.
The Bird, the other girl, Emily, said I will get my shoebox.
The Bird, we tried to get her warm and dry,
But she was frozen and she died.
The Bird, it was her time to go to "Birdie Heaven."

The Bird That Gets Eaten

The Bird That Gets Eaten, we went to take the bird that died the night before.
The Bird That Get Eaten, there were feathers everywhere and Emily was crying because of it.
The Bird That Get Eaten, something ate the bird was it a dog or was it a cat, or something else?
The Bird That Get eaten, that was so sad, blood everywhere! It was like a sad feather walk.

New People

New people could be bad people.
New people could teach you new things.
New people could be the one to set you up.
New people could be good people.
New people could show you new things.
New people, cannot trust them.
New people could be here when you need help, to help.
New people that you meet.
New people, some are good and caring.
New people, some are bad and don't care.
New people, you learn new things.
New people, you eat new foods.
New people, learning different cultures.

Dare

Dare to live.
Dare to try new foods.
Dare to try something new.
Dare to try to see the world.
Dare to try and see other people for their side.
Dare to try and see and learn new things and people.

Believe in yourself and all the doors you need open will open.
When it is your time to go through,
When **God** wants you to do it, you will.
So do not give up on yourself, keep going on the road of life
And you will get there.

My baby girl, Lady. She keeps me going, she keeps me in line.

The Husband

The husband does the work outside the home.
The husband does his best in making the whole family happy.
The husband does his job to teach his children **God**.
The husband does take time to spend time with the wife.
The husband does the job of making sure everything is right.

The Path

The Path, the way some people go.
The Path, the way some people want to go.
The Path, the way some people want to get out of.
The Path, the way to go that is good.
The Path, the way to go is bad.
The Path, the way to go with **God**.
The Path, the way that you think you are cool, but not.

Think Big

Think Big, see things for what they are.
Think Big, see your life for what you want to see in it.
Think Big, see and try all kinds or places and things.
Think Big, see and smell the roses and really don't just say it
Think Big, see and take time for a lunch on the grass and see the birds flying and singing.

The Battle

The Battle; of life
The Battle; of test you go thru
The Battle; of good
The Battle; of evil
The Battle; of truth
The Battle; of doing bad things
The Battle; of doing good things

A Winner

A Winner is someone that lives with being raped.
A Winner is someone that lives with loss of family.
A Winner is someone that lives with trying to stay clean in today's world.
A Winner is someone that lives with mental health and wants to be right and do right but is hard.
A Winner is someone that lives with schizophrenia.
A Winner is someone that lives with bipolar disorder.
A Winner is someone that lives with alcoholism.
A Winner is someone that lives with being homeless.
A Winner is someone that lives with no one but can understand them
A Winner is someone that lives with feeling hopeless in their life.
A Winner is all of us that made it through our battles in life.

JONNA

I know God made you an angel. I miss you so much, you are with **God**. We miss you here, all of us - Missy

Things I Have Done In My Life

I have had five children. I had to give my third born son to **God** because he died. I have helped people when they needed it. I pray for people and families, and I rejoice and thank **God** when it comes to pass. I use to go to the nursing homes where we sang and read the **Word of God**, and spend time with them every Thursday in my earlier years.

I use to be one of the Christian 7 Support Team also back in my day; my name is Sister Melissa Carte, *the Prayer Warrior.*

I love everything in my life. I thank **God** and my family. I thank my grandpa for teaching me not to give up, that I can do it. For Steven helping me and showing what he knows. For all my children for giving me hope that I can do it. If they can, I can.

I love helping people, feeding people, and pray for people, and in my free time I make things to give for gifts at Christmas time.

And now, I am an Author with ASA Publishing Company.

All family and friends call me "Melissa".

The Small Story About Me

I was born in Monroe Michigan and I did not like school at first, but I did like it eventually. I like to make things and cook and spend time with baby pup, Lady Hill. I love God and it is because of Him that I got where I am today because of God. On the days I am at home, a good movie or a good book to read is nice.

I want to see people make it and not get lost in the rat race of life. Everyone has rights and need to know how to use them. **God bless you** on the road of life. Hope you get what you need on this road of life, **Do not let anyone tell you that you cannot make it, because you can, I did.**

May God be with you!

Last Page of My Book

Where did I get the poems from?
Real life.
And today's test that we go through,
The people that give me the will,
The hope and will to write is,

Jackie, Sylvia, Tammy, Emily, my grandpa, my grandma, my pup Lady, my family, my friends and the people that helped me in my time of need. I thank you all. I send all my prayers and love to all.

Greg,

We were always together at family outings.
You would get upset if I was left out and when someone would make fun of me.
You were always there for me like a brother.
You always watched over me.
I know in my heart that **God** made you an angel.
I came back to Monroe and you were gone.
I will love you always and miss you.

Love, Missy

Wednesday, February 23, 2011 75 cents

Driver killed when car slams into train

MONROE TOWNSHIP – Police believe a man drove around railroad crossing arms that had been lowered and was killed when his car was hit by a train on E. Dunbar Rd. east of S. Telegraph Rd. early this morning.

Monroe County sheriff's deputies identified the driver as Gregory A. Hopkins, 43, of Monroe. He was alone in the car and was pronounced dead at the scene.

Sgt. Brian Angerer said the accident happened about 4:45 a.m. Mr. Hopkins was driving a 1998 Buick Riviera west and proceeded to go around the gates when his car was hit by a southbound CSX freight train.

Police said the lights and bells were activated and the crossing arms were lowered at the crossing. The crumbled car came to rest on the shoulder of Dunbar next to the tracks. The victim was pinned in the wreckage and had to be freed by the Monroe Township Volunteer Fire Department.

The train stopped about a half mile down the tracks. The crossing was reopened around 8:15 a.m.

The victim lived in the Oakridge Estates mobile home park, deputies said.

It was the sixth fatality on Monroe County roads this year compared to two at this time in 2010.

Crews from Jim's Towing and CSX clear debris from the scene of a car-train accident at the tracks on E. Dunbar Rd. this morning.

– Evening News photo by KIM BRENT

2-25-11

Gregory Alan Hopkins

May 25, 1967-Feb. 23, 2011

Gregory Alan Hopkins was born in Monroe, Michigan, on May 25, 1967.

He was one of three children from the union of Benjamin Chester Hopkins and Sheilia Irene (Dusseau) Hopkins.

Gregory was baptized and received his First Communion at St. Anne Catholic Church. He had attended Monroe High School.

Gregory was married to the former Sheryl Riley.

For more than twenty years, he was employed as a commercial painter. Gregory was employed by several local companies as well as being independently employed for some time. He had also had worked for Bob Evans Restaurant as a cook. He took a medical retirement in 2006.

Gregory loved the outdoors, where he enjoyed fishing and bicycling. He also enjoyed shooting pool, drawing and sketching, and he had a passion for music and a love for playing his guitar.

Gregory had a gift with others as well. His personality was kind, caring, and helpful. He enjoyed bringing others happiness and laughter. Gregory had a great love for his family and friends, and was extremely proud of his children. He had great faith in his Lord and Savior and he received his strength from regularly reading his Bible.

Gregory Alan Hopkins, 43, of Monroe passed away from injuries suffered in a car accident on Wednesday morning February 23, 2011.

His passing was preceded by paternal grandparents, Rose Johnson and Chester Hopkins; and maternal grandfather, Kenneth Dusseau.

He leaves to cherish his memory two sons, Jasper (Nicole Roden) Hopkins of Southgate and Benjamin (Melissa) Robinson of Monroe; a granddaughter, Kira Grace Robinson of Monroe; his mother, Sheilia Hopkins of Monroe; his father, Benjamin (Juanita) Hopkins of Monroe; maternal grandmother, Wilma Dusseau; two sisters, Shawn Marie Besedich (Keith Guyot) of Dearborn and Cassandra Ann (Jeff) Perkins of Ida; one nephew, Steven Arthur Raymer; two nieces, Brandy Renee Raymer and Stephanie Nicole Hopkins; and great nieces, Gracianna Johnson and Aubrianna Johnson.

Friends may gather from 12:00 p.m. until 6:00 p.m., Saturday, February 26, at Merkle Funeral Service, 2442 N. Monroe St., (734) 384-5185. A celebration of his life will take place at 6:00 p.m. with the Rev. William Mossett pastor of St. Anne Catholic Church officiating.

In lieu of flowers, memorials are suggested to the wishes of the family or to Brain Trauma Injury Support.

Online words of inspiration and comfort can be made by visiting www.merklefuneralservice.com and then selecting the Life Stories page.

MISSING FAMILY AND FRIENDS?
THESE ARE WAYS TO HELP FIND THEM.
GOD BLESS YOU ALL IN LOOKING FOR THEM.

MISSINGPERSON.COM
MISSINGPERSON .HTM
USAPEOPLESEARCH.COM
GOVT-FILES.COM
WWW.PERSONSMISSING.ORG
CONSUMERS-GUIDE.ORG
WWW.MISSINGPEOPLE.NET
WWW.MISSINGKIDS.WS
WWW.NMCO.ORG
WWW.PEOPLESITE.COM

Made in the USA
Columbia, SC
31 March 2024